All-Sorts Prayer 2

Interactive prayers for all ages

Claire Benton-Evans

kevin mayhew

kevin mayhew

First published in Great Britain in 2011 by Kevin Mayhew Ltd
Buxhall, Stowmarket, Suffolk IP14 3BW
Tel: +44 (0) 1449 737978 Fax: +44 (0) 1449 737834
E-mail: info@kevinmayhewltd.com

www.kevinmayhew.com

ISBN 978 1 84867 432 5
Catalogue No. 1501305

Cover design by Rob Mortonson
© Image used under licence from Shutterstock Inc.
Edited by Claire Musters
Typeset by Richard Weaver

Printed and bound in Great Britain

To the many talented people with whom I have worked
on the following all-age, all-sorts services:

Open Door at St Margaret's, Northam
Second Sunday at St John's, Ivybridge
'It's church, Jim, but not as we know it' at St Thomas', Camelford
Tea at Tetha's at St Tetha's, St Teath

With special thanks to John, Chris and Jim
for letting us loose on their congregations.

Contents

About the author

Claire Benton-Evans writes exclusively for Kevin Mayhew and works as an all-age worship consultant, helping churches to devise fresh, dynamic worship for all ages. She also leads quiet days and workshops on creative prayer, interactive storytelling and children's spirituality. She studied at Oxford before teaching English and Drama in London, North Devon and Cornwall. The creative arts inspire her, exclusion makes her angry and family life keeps her feet on the ground. She likes empty beaches, good food, live theatre and the Greenbelt festival. She lives with her husband – a Church of England minister – and three children in North Cornwall.

Full details of Claire's books can be found on her website at:
www.clairebentonevans.com

Introduction

Why do we need 'all-sorts' prayers?

These prayers have been designed for use in any church service of any size, where the youngest people present are babies and toddlers and the oldest may be in their nineties. It could be a regular Family Service or a special occasion, such as a baptism or a Crib service. Perhaps there is a group of teenagers and a collection of school-age children with their parents. One church I know well is regularly attended by teenagers from a local special school who come in hi-tech wheelchairs with their carers. All have profound physical disabilities and, in many cases, associated learning difficulties, but they choose to come to church and two of them have been confirmed. In such a gloriously mixed gathering there will undoubtedly be people who are not used to church and who find our ways rather strange.

One of the many challenges presented by such a service is this: how can we gather these different people together in prayer in a way that engages them all? In an 'all-sorts' congregation, which is not only all-age but also includes different abilities and all kinds of church experience, we risk praying *at* some of these people instead of *with* them, giving them the idea that prayer is something which is done to them, rather than something that they may freely and actively engage in. If we are truly a Church that believes itself to be one body, then our corporate prayer should leave no one on the outside, looking in. In the words of a well-known collect, our prayers should gather together 'all sorts and conditions'[1] of people.

I have been exploring the challenge of all-sorts prayer since parenthood changed my own experience of church-going completely. Once I was able to sit, pew-bound and prayerful, for the length of a service; then I became a distracted manager of three small children in a variety of churches and, later, an all-age worship leader with my three (mostly) willing helpers. My fellow all-age leaders have been creative people, blue-sky thinkers, musicians and pragmatists, resourceful Sunday school leaders and imaginative clergy. Over the years they have

1. *Collect or Prayer for all Conditions of Men* in Prayers and Thanksgivings, BCP.

generously shared their ideas and congregations, encouraging me to develop my own all-sorts prayers and to try them out Sunday by Sunday. What began as an attempt to involve children in prayer has become a desire to help everyone discover creative and interactive ways of praying. The prayers in this book and in the first *All-Sorts Prayer*[2] are the result of this experimentation. They have been designed with the all-age, all-sorts church service in mind, but are equally adaptable for use in Sunday Schools, confirmation classes, youth clubs and house groups. My aim is to offer a varied and tempting assortment so that clergy, readers and lay leaders can pick and mix these all-sorts prayers to suit particular services and occasions.

What is different about these prayers?

At the heart of these prayers is a longing to use fewer words and more symbols, space, movement, stillness, sound and silence; a desire to respond to God with our bodies and all our senses as well as with the spoken word. There is now a growing understanding that this kind of prayer is a natural expression of children's spirituality.[3] The more I lead people of all ages in such prayer, the more I am convinced that adults too need interactive, sensory and creative ways to pray. Just because we are grown-up, we are not pure spirit and reason: we are also physical, emotional, imaginative, intuitive creatures who, like children, may respond to God in many different ways.

These prayer actions also suit different abilities, because they do not depend on the capacity to read or speak, or on intellectual comprehension. I have used several of them with the disabled teenagers with learning difficulties who came to church with their carers, and they all held seeds, tasted fresh bread, listened to the sound of a singing bowl. Such symbols, actions and sensory experience engaged them in prayer along with the rest of the congregation.

2. Kevin Mayhew, 2010.
3. This new understanding of children's spirituality has found expression in Godly Play, through its visually stimulating storytelling and the exploratory 'wondering' it encourages. More generally, there is now a growing interest in praying imaginatively with children, as shown by the hands-on, creative prayers of the Messy Church movement. See Jerome Berryman, *Godly Play*, Augsburg Books, 1995 and Lucy Moore, *Messy Church*, BRF, 2006 or www.godlyplay.org.uk and www.messychurch.org.uk. See also *Through the Eyes of a Child*, ed. Anne Richards and Peter Privett, Church House Publishing, 2009.

A poet once said that poetry 'can communicate before it is understood'.[4] It is equally true that God reaches out to us and communicates with us in ways that are felt or sensed before our rational brain is able to process what has happened. Prayer is about communication: whenever and however we pray, we open up a channel of communication between ourselves and God. If we want to grow more receptive to God then all of us, regardless of age and understanding, need to use as many channels as we can. This book offers a wide variety of accessible ways in which we may tune in to God.

The structure of the prayers

Each of the prayers in this book follows the same easy-to-use format, with the sections described below.

Resources

Each prayer begins with a resources list so that it is easy to see at a glance exactly what is required for a particular prayer. As these prayers are designed to be active, creative and appealing to the senses, many require several resources. Most of these are readily available in churches and Sunday Schools; others should be easy to find in local shops. The CD-ROM contains photocopiable resources. I have given as much information as possible to help you track down more specialised items: the internet is usually your best source, so be sure to allow enough time for your order to arrive. Wherever possible, try to provide the best-quality resources you can afford, because good materials show that we value people enough to give them the best we have. If the pens don't work and the felt is tatty, what does that say to people of any age who are trying to use these things in prayer?

Leaders

These prayers all come with a leader's script that takes you through the prayer from beginning to end. Clergy and experienced worship leaders may well choose to adapt this for their own purposes, but it is there to make these prayers easy for everyone to use, straight off the page. The script is for the busy minister who wants to see at a glance

4. T. S Eliot, 'Dante' (essay), 1929.

how the interactive Mothering Sunday prayer will work; for the nervous volunteer who has never led prayers before, as well as for the experienced Sunday School leader who wants to become more confident in leading non-verbal prayer.

Prayer action

While these prayers are introduced with some explanation and direction, the praying itself is usually non-verbal. Some of the prayer actions explore new ways of using familiar church resources such as candles, bells and broken bread. Many more have been inspired by surprising things: who would have thought that feathers, mirrors, ping-pong balls, sand and After Eight mints could be used in prayer? These refreshingly different prayer actions engage with the ordinary stuff of everyday life: they suggest that prayer is not a special activity for Sundays, but an integral part of our daily lives.

Closing words

In using non-verbal ways of praying, we nevertheless need something to mark the end of the prayer. Often a simple 'Amen' is enough, but sometimes I have found that a few words, spoken aloud, help to focus and underline the prayer that has been offered. These closing words do not supplant the prayer action: they simply offer another channel of communication. To use an example from the kind of all-sorts church service I described at the beginning, if the prayer action has involved lighting sparklers around an Easter bonfire (*Sparklers*, p.103), then for a toddler, his incandescent scribble in the air might be the shape of his prayer. For the disabled teenager, it may be the experience of joining a circle of people and watching the fizzing light of the sparklers. For the elderly widow, the description of the sparklers as 'beacons to celebrate the good news of Easter' might be at the heart of her prayer.

In the end, the leader's introduction and the closing words are simply brackets enclosing a space in which prayer is offered by each individual. It is a space in which God is waiting for us, a space that is full of his love and alive with the communicating action of his go-between Spirit.

Why an *All-Sorts Prayer 2*?

In *All-Sorts Prayer*, I began to explore the possibilities of prayer beyond the traditional hands together, eyes closed and lots of words with 'Amen' at the end. As more churches become used to different ways of praying, they may settle on certain forms of interactive prayer with which people are comfortable. It is now just as important for congregations to discover that not every all-age prayer requires pebbles, salt dough or felt pens. The prayers in this book are divided into different categories to help worship leaders introduce a variety of ways of praying, by using – for example – music in one service, a creative response the next and a sensory prayer the following month. The biggest section is called 'Praying where we are'. It offers a selection of interactive prayers which do not require people to move around – this in response to the complaint I have heard most often from all-age worship leaders: 'People don't like getting up out of their seats!' Most of the prayers in this book can be adapted so that people can pray in their places, but the 'Praying where we are' section is especially for those people who physically can't get up easily during a service – and for those congregations who simply won't!

This book also includes a fresh selection of seasonal prayers for the church's special occasions. These often bring unusually large numbers of people to our churches, and many of them will come as families. Our feasts and festivals are wonderful opportunities for introducing all sorts of prayers to all sorts of people.

Active prayers

Children who are new to church, and their parents, often worry that a church service is all about sitting still and being quiet. These active prayers are one way of demonstrating that this need not always be the case. There are times when stillness and quietness are called for in church, but there can also be activity – even noise and mess!

These active prayers are also a useful reminder that in many Christian traditions, church is a place of movement, dance, general hubbub or ecstatic cries. My favourite example is St Dominic, who 'found it soothing after a long day's working or travelling to go into church and leap up and down, genuflecting with tremendous agility, until he was drawn into more tranquil prayer.'[5] If Christians down the ages and across the world have found active forms of prayer helpful, then maybe they are something for all of us to try, fidgety children and sedentary grown-ups alike.

5. Simon Tugwell, *Prayer in Practice*, Veritas Publications, 1974, p.29.

New life

Resources
- Lots of easy-to-grow flower seeds, suitable for planting at this time of year
- A tray full of potting compost, for starting the seeds off inside

Leader
Jesus offers us forgiveness for everything we have done wrong; he offers us new life. All we have to do is say sorry to God. As we pray today, we will bury these seeds in this soil as a sign that we are prepared to leave behind our old ways and receive new life in Christ. In a moment of quiet, let's call to mind all those things for which we need to say sorry.

Pause.

Now let's plant these seeds as a sign of our repentance and our prayer for new life.

Prayer action
Invite everyone to come forward and sow a seed in the tray.

Closing words
Heavenly Father,
in your love may you bury the wrong
we have done,
the unkind words we have spoken
and the messes we have made.
We are truly sorry.
May we grow in newness of life
in Jesus' name,
Amen.

Keep the seeds well-watered on a sunny window-sill. When they have grown into seedlings, you could either divide them for people to take home or plant them outside your church.

Turning the tables

Resources

- Around the church, display pictures and information about our world that highlight inequality and injustice [6]
- Paper and pens
- A lightweight table, placed at the front of church

Leader Today we will pray for change. We remember when Jesus shouted about the need for change: the temple in Jerusalem was being used as a market rather than a place of prayer, and Jesus was so angry that he overturned the stalls and moneylenders' tables. All around our church today are pictures and information about our world that show the need for change. Take your time to find out as much as you can.

Allow plenty of time for people to take in all the information.

Let's bring to this table any situation that we feel needs to change: you may like to bring one of the pictures or pieces of information that you have just looked at, or you may like to write or draw something of your own. Whatever it is that needs to change, bring it forward and lay it on this table.

6. Many resources can be downloaded from the internet, or obtained directly from organisations and charities such as the United Nations, Amnesty International, the Fairtrade Foundation, Traidcraft, Oxfam, Christian Aid, Save the Children and many others. Look for eye-catching pictures and keep the information simple, factual and relevant: for example, give the number of people in the world who live on less than a dollar a day; state what proportion of the world's population has no access to clean water; find out how long the waiting list for affordable housing is in your area.

Prayer action

Allow plenty of time for people to bring their prayers forward. You may like to invite some children to remain with you at the front to help push the table over.

As we look at the prayers spread out on this table, let us pray:

Temple-clearing Lord,
make us agents of change in your name.
May we, too, turn the tables.

Tip the table right over, so that all the papers scatter on the floor.

Closing words

Give us courage to challenge the way things are,
and determination to create a more just and
peaceful world.
Amen.

Taking up the cross

Resources

- Little pieces of paper, enough for one each
- Pens and pencils
- Small crosses – palm crosses would be ideal

Leader Jesus said, 'If any of you want to become my followers, you need to deny yourselves and take up your cross and follow me.'[7] In preparation for our prayers today, let's consider whether there is any part of ourselves, our attitudes or behaviour that is getting in the way of following Jesus. Is there anything in our lives that makes it hard for us to be loving and forgiving? As we call to mind whatever it is that we would like to leave behind us, let's write or draw it on one of these little pieces of paper.

Allow time for everyone to do so.

For our prayers today, you are invited to come forward and leave behind whatever is like an obstacle in your life. Scrunch it up, throw it down and pick up a cross instead, as a reminder that Jesus is calling you to go his way from now on.

Prayer action Encourage everyone to come forward and throw their scrunched-up piece of paper before the altar, or table, then take a small cross.

7. Adapted from Mark 8:34.

Closing words

Lord Jesus,
help us to leave our old ways behind us
and call us to follow you.
Though we are uncertain, guide us.
Though we are afraid, comfort us.
Though we are weak, give us strength.
Though we are doubtful, give us faith.
Though we may get lost, lead us home.
Amen.

Christ be with me

Resources
- Lit candles all around the church, on side tables and window-sills, each one with a few unlit tea lights clustered around it
- Matches and tapers

Leader
Jesus is always with us, wherever we are. As we pray together today, we will light candles all around the church to remind us that Jesus' love surrounds us. Can you find a lit candle and then look for an unlit one nearby? Light it where it is so that the candlelight starts to spread around the church.

Prayer action
Turn the lights off. Allow enough time for everyone to find and light a candle, then return to their seats.

Closing words
Jesus, as your light fills this church, we pray for your presence to fill our lives.
Christ be with us, Christ within us,
Christ behind us, Christ before us,
Christ beside us, Christ to win us,
Christ to comfort and restore us;
Christ beneath us, Christ above us,
Christ in quiet, Christ in danger,
Christ in hearts of all that love us,
Christ in mouth of friend and stranger.[8]
Amen.

8. Ascribed to St Patrick (372–466), trans. Cecil Frances Alexander (1818–95). Slightly adapted here.

Breaking down the barrier

Resources

- Small wooden bricks: the ones that make up the tower-building game, Jenga, are ideal
- Cross

Leader

For our prayers today, we will think about the walls we build between ourselves and God. He reaches out to us in love, but too often we block him out with walls that are built up out of our own wrongdoing and weakness. In a moment of quiet, let's remember all those things for which we need to say sorry.

Pause.

Before we ask for God's forgiveness together we will offer a sign that we are truly sorry. When you are ready, please come forward and add a brick to this wall. As you do so, say sorry to God in your heart.

Prayer action

Lead people in building a wall of wooden bricks in front of the cross on the altar or table, then stand behind the cross. You may like to invite people to gather round.

Let us pray.
Forgiving Lord,
we are sorry for the walls we have built
with these stumbling blocks.
May your renewing love
burst through this barrier of sin.

Push the cross forward so that it breaks down the wall of bricks.

Closing words

Draw us closer to you
in Jesus' name.
Amen.

Creative prayers

These prayers involve simple craft activities that are always popular in all-age services with lots of children. In this collection I have moved away from creative responses involving drawing or salt dough, with which congregations are becoming increasingly familiar: instead, here are prayers that look like ransom notes or paper trees. They offer fresh and surprising ways of responding to God.

These prayers are not just for the arty and crafty among us: they are designed to include those who have no artistic skill or inclination at all. I like the term my young daughter coined: they are 'making and doing' prayers that I hope will engage people of all ages and abilities.

Cut-out confessions

Resources

- Lots of glossy magazines and advertising material such as flyers, brochures and catalogues
- Scissors
- Glue sticks, PVA glue or Sellotape
- A5 pieces of card, enough for one each
- An example you have made earlier: an A5 piece of card with the letters spelling 'SORRY' cut out from magazines and stuck on, like a ransom note

Leader

For our prayers today we will say sorry to God. We will begin by looking at these glossy magazines and adverts, remembering how often our heads have been turned by the world's priorities. As we look through these shiny, colourful pages, let's call to mind all the attention we have given to money, to appearances and to material things. We need to ask God's forgiveness for the times we have been distracted from him. *(Pause)*. As a sign of our prayer, we will spell out the word 'Sorry' in letters taken from these pages. We will then come forward and offer these cut-out confessions to God.

Prayer action

Show your own 'Sorry' card and invite everyone to make their own by cutting and sticking individual letters. Place your own card on the altar or table and encourage everyone else to do the same when they are ready.

Closing words

O Lord,
forgive us for the times
we have been distracted from you
and dazzled by all that the world has to offer.
Help us to look to you
and put love first in our lives.
Amen.

Prayer plants

Resources

- By the altar or table, a tray prepared for the prayer plants *(see appendix, p.117)*
- Some tables, covered with the following: template for prayer plants (on CD-ROM, *see appendix, p.117*); pieces of green paper of varying sizes; Sellotape; scissors and pens

Leader

God's love is like a garden in which we can grow and change. Today we are going to make growing plants that we will use in our prayers.

Gather people around the tables and demonstrate how to roll, stick and cut the green paper, then make the 'plant' grow.

Before we each make a plant to use in our prayers today, let's think who we might pray for. You may know someone who wants to change, or who needs more space in their life to grow. You might know someone who is facing a big change in their life, such as a new home or school. Whoever you pray for, draw them or write their names in this space here. *(Indicate the box on the template.)* Then start to roll your paper from the opposite end.

Allow plenty of time for people to complete their prayer plants.

Now let's use our prayer plants to make a growing garden of prayer. Let us pray for all those who are facing change or longing to grow.

Prayer action

Encourage people to bring their plants forward and 'plant' them on the tray in front of the altar or table.

Closing words

Father God,
may your love be for all of us a fertile garden.
Tend us and nurture us
so that we might grow into our true selves.
Amen.

He holds us in his hands

Resources

- Under every seat: a pen and a large self-adhesive label: address labels are ideal
- Cards with cupped hands, enough for one each (on CD-ROM, *see appendix, p.117*)

Leader

Our prayer action today is inspired by a song: 'Our God is a great big God and he holds us in his hands'. Our God is a great, big, powerful God who can do amazing things. We don't need to be afraid because he holds us all in his hands. In a moment of quiet, let's rest in God's presence. Now let us call to mind the things that frighten us, and the situations we face in which we need his help and strength.

Pause for a short time.

Now let's take a moment to sign our names on one of these sticky labels. Then, as a sign of your prayer, please come forward and place your name in God's hands.

Prayer action

The people sign their names on the labels. Then they come forward to the altar, take a card showing the cupped hands and stick their self-adhesive signatures in the middle. Encourage them to take their cards home.

Closing words

Let us pray.
Great big God,
you are stronger than everything.
Hold us in your hands
today and always.
Amen.

X-ray specs

Resources

- Copies of the template on coloured A4 card (on CD-ROM, *see appendix, p.118*)[9]
- Scissors
- Sellotape

Leader

Jesus told his disciples to ignore appearances and look for goodness on the inside, not the outside.[10] His words apply to us, too: we need to look at what people are like in their hearts, as if we had a special kind of X-ray vision – and what we see there may surprise us. Today we will make these 'X-ray specs' as a reminder to look on the inside, not the outside.

Gather everyone around the craft tables and show them how to make the 'X-ray specs': cut out the glasses and the arms, fold back the tabs and attach the arms with Sellotape.

For our prayers today, we will make and wear our X-ray specs to remind us of God's different way of seeing.

Prayer action

People make their own pair of X-ray specs and then put them on. When everyone is ready, pause for a short time.

Closing words

Lord Jesus,
now we all look different!
You taught us to look at the world in a new way:
help us to see not the outside but the inside,
and to look for you in everyone we meet.
Amen.

9. You could try some different variations, for example: cut the glasses out of thin craft foam sheets and make the arms out of pipe cleaners, accessorise the glasses with stickers, stick-on jewels or sequins, stick on coloured cellophane lenses.
10. See Mark 7:1-23.

Prayer cube

Resources
- Net for the prayer cube, printed on A4 sheets of card (on CD-ROM, *see appendix, p.118*)
- Felt pens
- Scissors
- Double-sided sticky tape

Leader Someone asked Jesus, 'Which is the most important commandment?' He answered with words from the Old Testament which were known to every Jew: 'Hear, O Israel: The Lord is our God, the Lord alone. You shall love the Lord your God with all your heart, and with all your soul and with all your might.' There follows a special instruction: 'Keep these words that I am commanding you today in your heart. Recite them to your children and talk about them when you are at home and when you are away, when you lie down and when you rise. Bind them as a sign on your hand, fix them as an emblem on your forehead, and write them on the doorposts of your house and on your gates.'[11] Jewish people still do this today.

As a way of keeping this commandment close to us and part of our daily lives like this, we will make a prayer cube that we can keep at home where we will see it every day.

Show your prayer cube net and fold it up to form a box.

Keep your prayer cube on your kitchen table, by your bed or next to your toothbrush – anywhere where you will see it every day and be reminded that God is love and this *(show your cube)* is his most important commandment: 'You shall love

11. Deuteronomy 6:4-9, also in Mark 12:28-34.

the Lord your God with all your heart, and with all your soul, and with all your mind, and with all your strength.'

Prayer action — Invite everyone to cut out, colour and make their own prayer cube, then hold it in their hands.

Closing words — God of love,
we are yours, body and soul.
Make us always mindful of your love
and wholehearted in our love of one another,
in Jesus' name.
Amen.

Listening prayers

'We have two ears and only one mouth, so in our prayers we should listen twice as much as we talk.' This familiar statement is easy to repeat, but silent listening in prayer is hard. The writer, Sara Maitland, has documented her quest for silence and she describes it like this:

> The experience of most people who voluntarily take themselves off into silence is that it takes a while to settle into it. Of course, it does not grow more silent as time passes, but you do become more attuned to the silence. Unlike sound, which crashes against your ears, silence is subtle. The more and the longer you are silent the more you hear the tiny noises within the silence, so that silence itself is always slipping away like a tiny wild animal. You have to be very still and lure it. This is hard; one has only to try to quieten one's mind or body to discover just how turbulent they are.[12]

It may be that many children's apparent inability to sit still and be quiet in church is merely an outward, physical expression of this turbulence, which is common to all of us: who can say that their thoughts have never wandered during prayer? These listening prayers are designed to help all of us practise silence: some offer ways of settling into it and becoming attuned to the tiny noises within it; others may help us to focus on the silence, to lure it. In the silence, we wait for God.

12. Sara Maitland, *A Book of Silence*, Granta Books, 2008.

Candlelight

Resources • A candle and matches[13]

Leader *Invite people to sit in a circle around you. If your congregation is very large, just invite the children. Place an unlit candle in the middle.*

When we pray, it is good to remember that we have only one mouth but we have two ears, so we need to listen to God twice as much as we talk to him. For our prayers today we will sit in silence together for a short time and simply listen. This can be hard, but let's try and stay as quiet as possible. It helps to have something to look at, so when I light this candle, our silent, listening prayers will begin. When I blow it out, we will say together, 'Amen.'

Prayer action Light the candle and keep silence. If lots of very young children are present, it may be best to blow the candle out after about a minute.

Closing words **Amen.**

13. For a more ambitious period of silence, you could burn a single birthday candle down to nothing. This takes about ten minutes: it focuses the attention because the candle burns down almost imperceptibly, with hardly any wax drips. Push the candle through a small circle of card and hold it by the stub; if you want to reduce the burning time, push more of the candle through the card and leave only half of it to burn, or less.

Seashell

Resources

- A fairly large seashell, suitable for listening to the sound of waves

Leader

If we are to hear what God is saying to us when we pray, we need to practise listening. This doesn't just involve our ears: listening to God means paying attention, holding our minds and hearts open to receive his word. Our prayers today will help us practise paying attention to God.

Show the large seashell.

When we are young, we learn to listen for the sound of the sea in a seashell like this. It is wonderful to catch the swoosh of waves in your ear. As preparation for our listening prayers today, we will pass this shell around and begin by listening for the sound of the sea inside it. When you have heard it, pass the shell on, but hold on to the feeling you had when you were listening hard: that same experience of being quiet, staying still and paying attention is what we need to use in prayer. As we pass the shell around, let's remember how to rest in God's presence and pay attention to him.

Prayer action

Pass the shell around until everyone has settled into silence and stillness.

Closing words

Heavenly Father,
we offer you our quiet attention.
In the midst of our noisy world,
may we remember how to listen to you.
Amen.

Sound and silence

Resources
- Loud, upbeat music and equipment to play it on

Leader
We live in a noisy world. We are so surrounded by loud music, beeping machines and electronic devices that it can often be hard to find the silence we need in order to listen to God. In music, a moment of silence is called a rest. We will begin our prayers today with music: then we will rest in silence. When the music stops, make yourself comfortable and rest quietly in God's presence.

Prayer action
Play the music loudly. People can move around, dance or sing along as it plays. Suddenly stop the music and wait for people to settle into silence. Pause for a short time of quiet.

Closing words
God our Father,
give us rest from the sounds which fill our ears
so that we might hear your still, small voice.
Amen.

Rest

Resources

- Create some 'comfort zones' in church where people can relax: for example, areas with a small tent, rugs and cushions, deckchairs and sun loungers or beanbags and blankets
- *(Optional)* A short piece of instrumental music and equipment to play it on

Leader

The sabbath is a day of rest: it is a day for refreshing ourselves and refocusing our lives on God. Our recreation is also 're-creation' because it allows us to make a new start. As part of that renewal, we need to pay attention to God in our lives and listen afresh for his call. For our prayers today, you may like to settle yourself in one of these comfort zones or you can simply remain where you are. Let's take some time now to rest quietly in God's presence and listen to him.

Prayer action

Allow time for people to get comfortable and settle into quietness. You may like to play the music during this time of prayer.

Closing words

Lord of the sabbath,
may you make us new.
We come with faults and failings;
may you forgive us.
We come as broken, suffering people;
may you make us whole.
We come with gladness;
receive our thanks.
We come with wandering attention;
call us by name.
We come with heads full of noise;
grant us your peace.
Amen.

Bell

Resources • A singing bowl or large bell [14]

Leader When we pray, we don't need to worry about what to say to God. Listening to him is enough. Our listening prayer today will begin with the ringing of this singing bowl/bell. Let's listen as the note fills the air; then, as we try to catch the last of the fading sound, let's keep on listening. Let's wait for God in the silence.

Prayer action Ring the singing bowl or bell and let the note fade. Pause for a short time.

Closing words Loving Lord,
in our quietness
we share with you
the silence of eternity
interpreted by love.[15]
Amen.

14. The singing bowl is used as a meditation aid in Eastern religions. It may be found in shops that sell clothing and ornaments from India and the Far East. It looks like a metal pestle and mortar. You rub the outside rim of the bowl with the wooden beater, firmly and slowly, and a bell-like note wells out of the bowl, growing and fading as you 'stir' the sound. Ask for a demonstration in the shop! It requires some practice, but the effect is startling and unearthly. See my website www.clairebentonevans.com for a picture and further information.
15. From J. G. Whittier, 'Dear Lord and Father of mankind'.

Mark-making prayers

However we pray, many of us find it helpful on occasion to write our prayers down. I think of the urgent petitions pinned to the statues of saints in some Roman Catholic churches; the scraps of paper covered in Hebrew that are tucked between the stones of the Western Wall in Jerusalem; the books that rest by side altars in many of our churches, full of often anonymous prayers in different handwriting. Perhaps writing feels more substantial and permanent than speech: whatever the reason, it is clear that many different people share a deep need to offer prayers that leave their mark.

The following prayers involve written responses of different kinds. I have called this 'mark-making' because, in the interests of all-age inclusivity, the response could also be a drawing or simple marks with a crayon.

Water jars

Resources

- Pictures of stone water jars (on CD-ROM, *see appendix, p.118*)
- A collection plate
- Pens and pencils

Leader

Jesus performed his first miracle at a wedding party, when humble stone jars were filled with water *(show a small picture)* which then became miraculous wine. He showed that God understands our human needs and may respond in unexpected or surprising ways. In our prayers today we will take some time to bring before God our own concerns, however ordinary they may seem, trusting that he knows what we need. Let's take some time now to write or draw our prayers on these jars.

Prayer action

Allow plenty of time for people to complete their prayers; then gather them in a collection plate and bring them up to the altar or table.

Closing words

Lord of all goodness,
we place these prayers in your hands,
trusting in your transforming power.
Amen.

Questions

Resources

- A board with the outline of a cross drawn on it, placed in front of the altar or table
- A question mark card under every seat (on CD-ROM, *see appendix, p.118*)
- Pens and pencils
- Drawing pins

Leader

In our prayers we can come to Jesus as his disciples often did, with faith in our heart and questions on our mind. Let's take a moment now to call to mind any questions that we are carrying inside us. They may be big questions or niggling queries: whatever they are, write or draw one or two of them on these cards *(hold one up)* so that we can offer them to God in prayer. He may not answer our questions in the way we expect, and the response may be a long time coming, but in faith we can leave all our questions in his hands.

Prayer action

Allow plenty of time for people to write their questions. Invite people to bring their cards forward and pin them onto the cross.

Closing words

Let us pray.
Jesus, in this time of quiet,
we bring you our questions.
We leave them in your hands.
Amen.

Bright and beautiful

Resources
- Shaped cards representing different aspects of God's creation (on CD-ROM, *see appendix, p.119*)
- Felt pens, pens and pencils

Leader
All around us is the beautiful world that God made for us. We tend to take it for granted, but in our prayers today we will have an opportunity to pause, wonder and say, 'Thank you,' to God. Choose one of these shaped cards for your prayer: you could write or draw on it, or simply colour it in as a sign of your thanksgiving.

Prayer action
Allow time for people to choose their prayer shape and write or draw on it. Then encourage them to bring their prayers up to the altar or table, and spread them out in front of it.

Closing words
Almighty God,
thank you for your creation.
Help us to remember that from atoms to galaxies,
bacteria to blue whales,
daffodils to orang-utans and us –
everything is the work of your hands
and a sign of your glory.
Amen.

The worry box

Resources

- A cardboard box covered in white paper, with a cross on the front and a letterbox slot cut in the cross beam
- Small pieces of paper
- Pens and pencils

Leader

Many schools have a 'worry box' in which children can post the concerns they don't want to voice out loud. Our prayers can be a kind of worry box, too: we can share with God the worries, doubts and fears that we don't want to tell anyone else. In your own time, write or draw whatever concern you would like to share with God. We will post our prayers into this special box, which is marked with the symbol of God's love for us. Let's leave all our worries at the cross, in God's care.

Prayer action

Allow plenty of time for people to write or draw their prayers, fold them up and post them into the box.

Closing words

Let us offer all these worries to God.

Heavenly Father,
your love is greater than our fears,
your truth is deeper than our questions,
your everlasting life is stronger than our doubts.
Help us to leave these things in your hands
and trust in you.
Amen.

Lost sheep

Resources

- A large picture of Jesus, the good shepherd (on CD-ROM, *see appendix, p.119*), displayed on a board in front of the altar or a table
- Cards with the outline of a lamb (on CD-ROM, *see appendix, p.119*)
- Blu-tack
- Pens and pencils

Leader

Jesus called himself the good shepherd. The good shepherd is especially careful of his weakest lambs: he nurtures those who are sick or injured and those who are rejected. In our prayers today, we will remember anyone known to us who particularly needs the good shepherd's tender love and care at the moment. You are invited to write their name or draw them on these pictures of lambs, then come forward and add them to the good shepherd's flock.

Prayer action

Allow plenty of time for people to write their prayers and bring their lamb forward to add to the picture.

Closing words

Jesus, you are the good shepherd.
May your love enfold these lambs,
keep them safe and make them whole again.
Amen.

Praying with music

Praying with music is an ancient tradition that, in Christianity, reaches back to plainsong and beyond. In an all-age context, we can explore a wide range of music: for example, there have been popular experiments such as the U2charist – a Communion service featuring music by the rock band, U2 – and even a *Glee*charist, with songs from the popular TV series. If we are looking to engage people of all ages in prayer and worship, then we need to use all kinds of music that they know and love.

The following prayers cover a range of musical genres: pop, folk, Taizé chant, modern worship music and sung prayer from the sixteenth century. They also involve different kinds of interactivity, from singing to simple actions.

Be still

Resources

- Large candle
- Lots of tea lights
- Under every seat: a thin votive candle, preferably with a cardboard disc to protect hands from dripping wax
- Matches and tapers
- Words for 'Be still, for the presence of the Lord'
- Two singers

Leader

Today we will pray with music and action. Let's be still in the presence of the Lord, remembering that he is always with us.

Prayer action

Begin in darkness. The first singer walks down the aisle carrying the large lighted candle and singing the first verse, 'Be still, for the presence of the Lord'. Meanwhile, the second singer is laying out radiating lines of unlit tea lights on the floor at the front of church. By the end of the verse, the large candle is placed in the centre of the tea lights.

Both singers sing the second verse, 'Be still, for the glory of the Lord,' as they light the tea lights that radiate from the large candle.

Everyone sings the last verse, 'Be still, for the power of the Lord,' as the singers pass among the people with lit tapers and light the votive candles. The light is passed from person to person until all the candles are lit. Pause for a short time at the end of the hymn.

Closing words

May God the Father watch over us,
may God the Son walk with us
and may God the Holy Spirit work in us
today and always.
Amen.

The Lord is my song

Resources
- Laptop, projector and screen
- Slideshow based on Psalm 147 [16]
- Words for the Taizé chant 'The Lord is my song'

Leader: For our prayers today we will use some words of praise from one of the Bible's songs, which are known as Psalms. Each verse has a picture to help us think about how good our God is. In between each verse and picture we will sing God's praises with a simple chant: 'The Lord is my song'. Let us pray.

Prayer action: Alleluia.
How good it is to make music for our God,
how joyful to honour him with praise.
The Lord is my song . . .

(Show picture of someone comforting a distressed person.)

He heals the broken-hearted
and binds up all their wounds.
The Lord is my song . . .

(Show picture of a night sky full of stars.)

He counts the number of the stars
and calls them all by their names.
The Lord is my song . . .

16. This version of the Psalm is from the *Common Worship Psalter* – you may prefer to use a different translation. The best computer programs for creating slideshows are PowerPoint for PCs and Keynote for Macs. Look on the internet for copyright-free images, for example at www.shutterstock.com. Your own photographs of wild and beautiful places in your local area can also be very effective here.

(Show picture of ocean waves.)

Great is our Lord and mighty in power;
his wisdom is beyond all telling.
The Lord is my song . . .

(Show picture of a cloudy sky with a rainbow.)

Sing to the Lord with thanksgiving;
make music to our God upon the lyre;
who covers the heavens with clouds
and prepares rain for the earth;
The Lord is my song . . .

(Show picture of green fields.)

who makes grass to grow upon the mountains
and green plants to serve our needs.
The Lord is my song . . .

(Show picture of praying hands.)

The Lord delights in those who fear him,
who put their trust in his steadfast love.
The Lord is my song . . .

Closing words **Amen.**

Down to the river to pray

Resources

- Flower petals in a bowl
- A large, shallow dish of water [17]
- Recording of 'Down to the river to pray' [18] plus equipment to play it on

Leader

In our prayers today we will remember all those who need to be made whole: the broken-hearted and all who suffer in body, mind or spirit.

Pause for a moment of quiet.

We pray for our broken world and for the suffering of those whose names we do not know.

Pause for a moment of quiet.

We will use these fallen petals as a sign of our prayer. As the music plays, come forward and cast your petals on the water.

Prayer action

Play the music. Pass round the bowl of petals and encourage people to come forward and cast them on the water.

Closing words

O Lord, hear our prayers
for the bruised and the broken,
in Jesus' name.
Amen.

17. This prayer could be used as part of an outdoor service in which the petals are cast on a pond or river.
18. Sung by Alison Krauss on the soundtrack album for *O Brother, Where Art thou?* (Various artists, Lost Highway, 2000).

God be in my head

Resources

- Words for 'God be in my head' (if possible, displayed on a screen)
- *(Optional)* An accompanying musician

Leader

Our prayer today reminds us that we need God at the forefront of our lives. At our right hand, in our head and heart, in what we say and in the way we look at the world, may God be always with us to guide us and show us which way to go.

Prayer action

You may like to encourage people to use actions in this prayer, touching head, eyes, mouth and heart in turn, then crossing hands over the heart for 'God be at mine end'.

Let us sing together and pray:
God be in my head,
and in my understanding;
God be in mine eyes,
and in my looking;
God be in my mouth,
and in my speaking;
God be in my heart,
and in my thinking;
God be at mine end,
and at my departing.

Closing words

Amen.

Sailing

Resources

- A recording of 'Sailing' sung by Rod Stewart, plus equipment to play it on
- Words for 'Sailing'

Leader

Jesus' first disciples were fishermen. They knew what it was like to be at the mercy of wind and waves; they knew how suddenly calm water could be whipped up by a storm. Life as Jesus' disciples turned out to be just as unpredictable.

When Jesus calls us to follow him, he calls us on a lifelong adventure which, like a sea voyage, can be risky, challenging and full of wonders. In our prayers today we will use a well-known song to bring before God our own journeys of discipleship. We pray that we might continually travel closer to him.

Prayer action

Play the recording of 'Sailing' and encourage everyone to join in.

Closing words

Father, call us home
to be near you,
to be with you,
to be free.
Amen.

Praying with gesture

Whether we choose to kneel, sit cross-legged, stand with arms upraised or lie face down on the floor, our physical position is an important part of the way we pray. Posture and gesture can be as eloquent as words. However, in traditional church services our prayers can seem somewhat separate from our physical selves, since our standing, sitting or kneeling is a matter of convention rather than spontaneous physical expression. The prayers in this section will help our all-age congregations make their praying a whole-body experience.

It is worth noting that several of these prayers need no resources. This makes them particularly suitable for a large congregation, or for an all-age service that already requires numerous resources for its storytelling and associated activities.

Whole body

Resources
- Joyful recorded music[19] and equipment to play it on
- Percussion instruments
- Worship flags and streamers[20]

Leader Our prayers today will give us an opportunity to praise God with our whole body. This is a moment for sharing with God our wonder, thanks and praise for whatever is good in our lives. Let's think about what we would like our prayer of praise to be.

Pause.

Now each of us can choose how to pray. You may wish to sit quietly and ponder God's goodness in your heart. You may want to be loud; you could even leap for joy or dance about with one of our worship flags or streamers! Alternatively you may simply want to stand still in wonder. We will have some joyful music to help our praises, and there are some musical instruments here if you would like to join in. Choose whatever you would like to do and move into an open space in the church if you need to. Our prayers will begin when the music starts.

Allow a moment for people to move or to collect instruments, worship flags etc.

Let us greatly rejoice in the Lord. May our whole being exult in our God!

19. Choose anything upbeat and celebratory, in any genre: worship songs (e.g. 'Sing to the Lord'); gospel (e.g. 'O Happy Day'); classical (e.g. the 'Hallelujah' chorus from Handel's *Messiah*) or secular pop music (e.g. Nizlopi's 'Sing Around It').
20. See Kingdom Dance Resources at www.kingdomdance.co.uk.

Prayer action
Start the music and allow people time and space to pray in whatever way they wish. As soon as the music finishes, say the closing words loudly and joyfully.

Closing words
Glory be to the Father, and to the Son and to the Holy Spirit!
Amen.

Body of Christ

Resources

- The words of the prayer, displayed on a screen or a large card

Leader

Our prayer today is an active prayer that will help us to think about how Jesus is active in the world today. When you hear the word 'body', cross your hands over your chest like this *(demonstrate action)*. When you hear the word 'hands', open your hands in front of you like this *(demonstrate action)*. When you hear the word 'feet', stamp your feet once like this *(demonstrate action)* and when you hear the word 'eyes', point to your eyes *(demonstrate action)*. Let's practise: *(do the actions together)* 'body', 'hands', 'feet', 'eyes', 'feet', 'hands'. Now listen closely for those words as we pray together:

Prayer action

Christ, you have no *body* now on earth but ours,
no *hands* but ours, no *feet* but ours.
Ours are the *eyes* through which your compassion is to look out on the world.
Ours are the *feet* by which you are to go about doing good,
and ours are the *hands* with which you are to bless us now.[21]

Closing words

Lord Jesus,
show us how to do your work in the world.
Amen.

21. Adapted from St Teresa of Ávila (1515-82).

Annunciation

Resources

This is a resource-free prayer that is particularly suitable for Advent and Christmas.

Leader

We need to practise some actions for our prayers today, which are inspired by Mary's encounter with an angel. When Gabriel told her that she would give birth to God's Son, he praised the coming of Christ's everlasting kingdom – like this.

Hold up your arms in an open gesture of praise and encourage everyone to do the same.

Mary wondered at the angel's message and asked, 'How can this be?'

Open your hands with a questioning shrug and encourage everyone to do the same.

Finally, Mary accepted God's will for her with the words, 'Here am I, the servant of the Lord; let it be with me according to your word.' She showed her obedience to God.[22]

Kneel down and encourage everyone to do the same, then stand up again.

We will use these three gestures – praise, questioning and obedience – in our prayers today. Let us pray.

22. Luke 1:26–38.

Prayer action

Heavenly Father,

Hold your arms up in an open gesture and encourage everyone to do the same.

You hold all possibilities in your hands
and nothing is impossible with you.
Make known your will for each one of us,
though we may ask, 'Who, me?'

Open your hands with a questioning shrug and encourage everyone to do the same.

Take us as we are and accept all that we have.

Kneel down and encourage everyone to do the same.

Closing words

Let it be with us according to your word.
Amen.

Inclusive circle

Resources: This is a resource-free prayer.

Leader: In God's love, there is no 'us' and 'them': his love includes us all. For our prayer today, we will form a circle that includes everyone but which faces outwards, to show we are always ready to let more people in.

Prayer action: Encourage everyone to spread out around the church and to join hands in one big outward-facing circle.

Closing words: Let us pray.

Loving Lord,
in your love, there is no 'us' and 'them', only yours.
For this welcoming love which leaves no one outside,
for this inclusion,
for this belonging,
we praise you.
Amen.

Words of my mouth

Resources This is a resource-free prayer.

Leader As we rest in God's presence today, we will think about our mouths and all the words that come out of them.

Pause.

We call to mind the unkind words we have said and the loving words we have failed to say; we bring before God the thoughtless words we have forgotten.

Pause.

We say sorry to God in our hearts for the words that have wounded others, by accident or on purpose. We ask God to forgive us.

Pause.

Prayer action Our prayer is one that ministers sometimes use before they preach. When I say the word, 'mouth', please make the sign of the cross with your finger over your lips.

Demonstrate this action and practise by saying, 'the words of our mouths', as everyone makes the sign of the cross.

When I say the word, 'heart', please make the sign of the cross with your finger over your heart.

Demonstrate this action and practise by saying, 'the meditation of our hearts', as everyone makes the sign of the cross.

Let us pray.

Let the words of our mouths
and the meditation of our hearts
be acceptable to you,
O Lord, our rock and our Redeemer.

Closing words **Amen.**

Sensory prayers

These prayers are particularly suitable for an all-sorts congregation because they do not rely on words or understanding. They simply appeal to the senses in order to open up an awareness of God's goodness. The power of such an appeal is suggested by this lovely description of a baby girl, Madeleine, being almost overwhelmed by the sensory experiences of her first birthday party:

> We had talked up the birthday to Madeleine, but it meant nothing to her. What mattered was . . . her first dessert, an apple bundt cake, with a single short, fat candle filling the hole in the middle. This was the first lit candle she had ever seen, and the mercury blob of flame was perhaps a laughing eye. She smiled at the candle and hid her face, as she did with strangers. The four adults singing in unison was an amazement, as though we all had become one person, channeling the voice of the air in the room. We tried to show her how to blow out the candle. She pursed her lips, but did not exhale. Did we want her to kiss it? She pursed her lips again while we blew, and the eye winked out. This disconcerted her, but she forgot everything in the apple cake, a revelation, a whole new world of possibilities opening before her.[23]

If a candle, singing and cake can provoke awe and wonder in this secular context, then what power might such simple things have to stimulate the prayers of our all-age congregations? The following prayers explore the sensory power of birdsong, fresh bread, clean water, colourful pictures and soft sand.

23. Brian Hall, *Madeleine's World: A Biography of a Three-Year-Old*, Secker and Warburg, 1998.

Water of life

Resources • Enough cups of water for the whole congregation

Leader *Give everyone a cup of water before you begin this prayer.*

Lord of life,
thank you for the running water
that sustains our bodies;
thank you for your living water
that saves our souls.
As we drink this water, we remember all those
who are thirsty in body, mind and spirit.

Prayer action Encourage everyone to drink the water together.

Pause.

Closing words We pray that they will find the water of life.
Amen.

Bread of life

Resources

- A loaf of warm, fresh bread that has been broken open so that the smell fills the air
- A plate

Leader

Gather your congregation in a circle around the altar or table. Hold the plate of fresh bread in front of you.

Jesus said, 'I am the bread of life. Whoever comes to me will never be hungry, and whoever believes in me will never be thirsty.'[24] For our prayers today, we will savour the warm, comforting smell of freshly baked bread. We remember all those who are physically hungry, and those whose heart, mind or spirit feels empty and unsatisfied.

Pause.

We pray for them and for ourselves. As we share this fresh bread, we say, 'Jesus is the bread of life.'

Prayer action

Take a piece of fresh bread and pass it to your neighbour. As you do so, say, 'Jesus is the bread of life.' The bread is then passed on in the same manner until the last person hands it back to you.

Closing words

Jesus, Bread of heaven,
feed us until we want no more.
Amen.

24. John 6:35.

Birdsong

Resources • Sound effect of birdsong [25]

Leader For our prayers today we will simply listen. As we hear the sound of birdsong, let's close our eyes and rest in the gentle music of God's creation. Let your own prayer gather in your heart as you listen.

Prayer action Play the birdsong and allow plenty of time for people to settle into quietness.

Closing words Creator God,
we thank you for this ever-evolving world,
for the diverse creatures sharing our earth,
sea and sky.
For the breathing spaces,
the green havens of peace
and the still waters that restore the soul,
we praise you, O Lord our God.
Amen.

25. Search the internet for free downloadable sound effects. For example, www.soundeffects.ch has some lovely long recordings under 'Birds, ambience': there is a four-minute track of general birdsong in a lakeside setting that would be ideal for this prayer.

Visual intercessions

Resources

- Small crosses, enough for one each[26]
- On the altar or table, spread four large, colourful, laminated pictures (either single images or montages) to represent the following: the Church; the world and/or those in power; your local community and those who suffer[27]

Leader

Today we will use pictures to help us pray.

Hold up the picture that represents the Church.

In a moment, we will pray for the Church: for our own congregation and leaders, and for churches across the world. Together, we are the Body of Christ.

Hold up the picture that represents the world and/or those in power.

We will pray for our world and for all those in positions of power, whose decisions change lives.

Hold up the picture that represents your local community.

We will pray for our local community.

Hold up the picture that represents those who suffer.

And we will pray for all those who suffer in body, mind or spirit.

In a moment of quiet, come forward and spend some time looking at these pictures. Then, as a sign of your prayer, place your cross on one of the pictures. Let us pray.

26. Palm crosses would be ideal. Alternatively, cut small crosses out of plain card.
27. Look on the internet for copyright-free images, for example at www.shutterstock.com. Pictures from newspapers or your own photographs of your church and community can also be very effective here.

Prayer action	Allow plenty of time for reflection as everyone comes forward and places their cross.
Closing words	Heavenly Father, on the cross your Son gave his life for the life of the world; so we offer these prayers in Jesus' name, **Amen.**

Grains of sand

Resources

- A tray of fine, soft sand, placed in front of the altar or table

Leader

In his goodness, God wants to pour his grace into our lives until it spills over the edges. We pray today that we may be ready to receive all that he has to give. We will use sand as a sign of our prayer because in the Bible, grains of sand are often compared to God's uncountable blessings. So we pour sand into each other's hands until it overflows and as we do so we say, 'May you be filled with all the fullness of God'.[28] The response is, 'Amen.'

Prayer action

Each person comes up in turn and pours sand into the next person's hands until it overflows into the tray below. Each time, the prayer and response is said.

Closing words

May we all be filled with all the fullness of God.
Amen.

28. From Ephesians 3:19.

Takeaway prayers

'Cause that's the way prayer do. It's like electricity.
It keeps things going.'[29]

These are the words of an African-American woman who prays every day, and her powerful description of prayer has made me think about different ways of encouraging people to continue praying. These 'takeaway' prayers offer ways of keeping things going, long after the service has finished: they give people something tangible to take away as a reminder of their prayer intention. The items are small and light, suitable for tucking into a purse or wallet. They may gather dust and be forgotten, but we never know when they might surprise us. I was recently rummaging for a receipt when I came across a silky piece of white ribbon: it was the symbol of Christ's forgiveness I had taken away from a Lent service[30] in which we nailed pieces of red ribbon to a large wooden cross as a sign of our sin and repentance. I remembered the physical effort and noise of hammering, and the sight of a six-foot wooden cross covered in scarlet. I remembered the confession I made and there in my hand was the white ribbon, the symbol of forgiveness I had received. If prayer is like electricity, then this experience convinced me that 'takeaway' prayers continue to be a live connection.

29. Kathryn Stockett, *The Help*, Penguin Books, 2010.
30. Critical Mass, devised by the Revd Paul Niemiec.

Mirror

Resources
- Small plastic mirrors, enough for one each[31]

Leader It is easy for us to point out what someone else has done wrong; far harder to take a long, hard look at ourselves. If we do, we discover that we are not perfect. All of us are trying to be the person God wants us to be, yet we often get things wrong. For our prayers today, we will use these little mirrors to help us turn our attention away from other people and consider ourselves, here in the presence of God. Don't focus on your appearance: look beyond it to think about what you are like on the inside. In a time of quiet, let's bring before God everything for which we are sorry: the things we have done and failed to do; the hurtful things we have said and the kind words we have left unspoken.

Prayer action Allow everyone to settle into silence, mirrors in hand. Give them space for reflection. Pause for a short time.

Closing words God of love,
you know us inside out.
We are sorry for all we have done wrong.
May you forgive our sins
so that our lives might reflect your glory.
Amen.

Please take your mirrors away with you and keep them in a purse or wallet. May they remind each of us to look at our lives and try to see ourselves as God sees us.

31. Thin, flexible plastic sheets with a mirror coating are available from craft stores. They are easy to cut into smaller pieces if necessary: 5cm x 2.5cm is a good size. For example, see the Mirror ten-pack at www.homecrafts.co.uk.

Mustard seed

Resources

- A bowl full of mustard seeds

Leader

Seeds are going to be the focus of our prayers today. *(Hold a seed in the palm of your hand.)* This mustard seed is a tiny packet of potential life. If we plant it and water it, then let nature do the rest, it will grow and become all that it can be. Mustard spreads like weeds and can even take over a garden. God's kingdom can grow like this, too: each kind word and good deed we sow has the power to take hold and spread. God's loving way of doing things is as strong, fast-growing and resilient as weeds.

As this bowl is passed around, take a mustard seed and hold it in your hands. Let's rest in God's presence and ask what we can do to help his kingdom take over the world.

Prayer action

Pass the bowl around until everyone has taken a seed.

Closing words

Heavenly Father,
send us out to grow your love in the world.
May you bless each seed we sow
and may your love take root and grow
until your kingdom comes.
Amen.

Take your mustard seed home and plant it on some damp kitchen roll. Leave it on a sunny window-sill, water it and, as you watch your seed grow, think what you might do to sow the seeds of God's kingdom.

Bloom

Resources

- A selection of different cut flowers. This prayer is particularly suitable for use during a flower festival: if each exhibitor donates a few spare blooms, you will have a beautiful variety to choose from

Leader

Jesus told his followers not to worry about their lives. He told them to look at the flowers and take heart, because God dresses them beautifully in all their exquisite colours, petals and fragrance, even though they are here for such a short time. If God lavishes such attention on these glorified weeds, Jesus argued, then how much more will he love and care for us, his people?[32] So, for our prayers today, we will consider the lilies, and all the other flowers we have brought into church. Come forward and choose a bloom, then let's take some time to wonder at the beauty of these flowers as we sit quietly in God's presence.

Prayer action

Everyone comes forward and chooses a flower, then contemplates it in silence.

Closing words

God, our Creator,
we thank you for the beauty of this green
and growing earth.
Like these flowers, we are the work of your hand;
may we grow strong in your watchful care
and trust in you.
Amen.

You may like to press your flower at home. Keep it to remind you of how God cares for his whole creation.

32. Matthew 6:28.

Feathers

Resources

- Lots of white feathers. For a good clean supply, I suggest taking apart a cheap feather-boa.

Leader

No one can say what God's Holy Spirit looks like. The Bible often describes the Spirit as a powerful wind: he comes and goes and, while you can't see him, you can feel his power and see the effects he has. Sometimes the Spirit appears as a dove, fluttering briefly down from heaven and perhaps leaving behind nothing but a feather or two to show where he's been.

Hold up a feather or two and let them drift down.

See how light and soft these feathers are! They are hardly there at all, yet they remind us of the bird whose powerful wings once beat the air. For our prayers today, we will use these white feathers to remind us that the Holy Spirit comes and goes in our lives, too. We may not see him, but we can feel his power and recognise him by the signs he leaves behind. Let's rest in God's presence and consider his Holy Spirit.

Prayer action

Invite everyone to take a feather or two and allow some time for people to sit quietly and consider them.

Closing words

Come, Holy Spirit,
fly down to us.
May we know you
by the inspiration and
transformed lives
you leave behind.
Amen.

Please take your feathers home with you. May they remind us all to look out for signs of God's Holy Spirit at work in the world and in our lives.

Gift

Resources

- Cards with a crown (on CD-ROM, *see appendix, p.120*), enough for one each and individually gift-wrapped
- A bowl for the wrapped cards

Leader

The kingdom of God is God's way of doing things, and that way is love. It is a gift that he gives to each one of us. For our prayers today, we will receive these gifts as a symbol of his kingdom. *(Hold up one of the gift-wrapped cards.)*

Prayer action

Everyone comes forward and receives a gift that they then unwrap to reveal a crown, labelled on one side, 'God's kingdom,' and on the other, 'LOVE is . . . God's way of doing things.'

Closing words

Our God and King,
help us to accept your way of doing things
and may your kingdom come.
Amen.

Please keep your card to remind you of what God's kingdom is all about.

Praying where we are

'This is my pew. This has always been my pew.'[33]

Many all-age worship leaders have admitted that they face the same challenge when it comes to using interactive prayers in their churches: 'People don't like having to move around!' It is fair to say that this is not always caused by the kind of attitude expressed above: many elderly people have mobility problems, and many older church buildings are awkward for anyone to negotiate with walking sticks, a frame or a wheelchair. These people may well be more comfortable with prayers that do not require them to move around.

There is another kind of service for which these prayers are particularly useful. If you are holding a large service in a cathedral, or if a special service in your church is unusually well-attended, then any kind of congregational movement is likely to be difficult and, above all, time-consuming. These prayers are designed to help your congregation pray both interactively and *in situ*.

33. Dave Walker cartoon, from *The Dave Walker Guide to the Church*, Canterbury Press, 2006.

Shoes

Resources — This is a resource-free prayer.

Leader — Paul tells Christians to put on 'the armour of God.' He specifically describes the different parts of this armour, such as the belt of truth and the shield of faith, but when he gets to the shoes he says only, 'put on whatever will make you ready to proclaim the gospel of peace.'[34] This business-like instruction reminds us that we have a job to do, and that job is to go and spread the good news about Jesus. He needs us to be armed, not for war, but for peace-making. Today we will pray an active prayer that we might be ready to do this; we begin by taking our shoes off.

Prayer action — *Pause while everyone does so, including you.*

Put your feet on the floor and notice how bare and vulnerable they feel without shoes. Let us pray.

Almighty God,
like our feet without shoes,
without you we are weak and exposed.
We pray that we may be strong
in the strength of your power.

Everyone puts on their shoes.

Like shoes for our feet,
may we put on whatever will make us ready
to proclaim the gospel of peace.

Closing words — We ask this in Jesus' name.
Amen.

34. Ephesians 6:10-17.

Lucky dip

Resources

- A cloth bag
- Lots of plain ping-pong balls,[35] enough for one each. Divide them into four batches and label them as follows, using a permanent marker: THANK YOU; PLEASE; SORRY and WOW!

Leader

Our prayers today will be a lucky dip! In this bag are lots of ping-pong balls. Each ball has a word on it to suggest a prayer. If you pick out a ball marked 'THANK YOU', thank God for something that is good in your life. If you pick out a ball marked 'PLEASE', yours will be an asking prayer: bring before God anyone who is in need. If your ball says 'SORRY', remember something that was your fault and ask God to forgive you. Finally, if your ball says 'WOW!', think of something amazing that God has made or done, and pray in awe and wonder. Let us pray.

Prayer action

Take a ball yourself and then pass the bag around the congregation. Once everyone has a ball, pause for a short time.

Closing words

Almighty God, your glory wows us into silence.

Pause.

We are sorry for the times we have let you down; may you forgive us.

Pause.

35. These are available in bulk fairly cheaply from sports shops and Amazon. Coloured balls would be lovely, but they are much more expensive than white. Whichever you buy, make sure they are completely plain: some have large brand names on them. Thanks to my son Tobias for the novel idea of 'lucky dip' prayers!

Please walk alongside those in need; may you give them strength.

Pause.

For all your great goodness, we say,
'Thank you, thank you, thank you, Lord.'
Amen.

Hurt

Resources

- A recording of 'Everybody Hurts' by R.E.M. (about 6 minutes long) and equipment to play it on

Leader

There are times when life is hard. When we have had enough, all we can do is come before God with our pain, hurt and sorrow. We can trust that he knows what we are going through because Jesus lived, suffered and died as one of us. Our God knows from bitter experience that everybody hurts, and so we are not alone in our struggles. He is with us.

Today we will use music in our prayers. As we listen, we may share our own hurt with God and remember all those known to us who are hurting.

Prayer action

Play the music, either to the end of the track or fading out part of the way through.

Closing words

Loving Father,
we bring our hurt before you
and place our brokenness in your hands.
May we know in our hearts
that your love surrounds us
and we will never be alone.
Amen.

Heart

Resources

- Lots of hearts cut out of red card or felt (on CD-ROM, *see appendix, p.120*)
- Collection plate or bowl

Leader

Our prayers today will use a sign that we all recognise. Who can tell me what this means?

Pass round the felt hearts and elicit the response, 'Love.'

The Bible is very clear about love. It says, 'God is love . . . The commandment we have from him is this: those who love God must love their brothers and sisters also.'[36] Loving our brothers and sisters means behaving in a kind and loving way not just to our siblings, but to all our fellow human beings. God is our loving Father and therefore we are all members of his family. It could be that we know a lonely person who needs a friend. Perhaps we need to make peace after a family row. Maybe someone we hardly know needs a kind word of encouragement.

Today we will use these symbols of love as a focus for our prayers. Hold your heart in your hands and, in a time of quiet, let's ask God to show us what we can do to love each other.

Prayer action

Pause for a short time.

Let's offer these hearts to God with a promise that we will show his love today in what we say and do.

Place your own heart in the collection plate, then pass the plate around so that everyone else can do the same.

36. 1 John 4:16, 21.

Closing words

Let us pray.

Father God,
in love you made us,
through love you saved us,
with love may we reach out to each other.
Amen.

VIP

Resources

- Conference badges, enough for one each. These are clear plastic badge holders with an attached clip or safety pin and space to hold a removable name card. Prepare the cards beforehand by printing 'VIP' at the bottom of each one, leaving enough space for someone's name above[37]
- Pens and pencils in every pew or row of seats

Leader

For our prayers today, we will use these name badges. Take one and slide out the little card, then write your name on it. The badge says 'VIP' because, to God, you are a Very Important Person.

Prayer action

Pause while everyone writes their name.

Let's take a moment to look at our own name badges and remember how special we are to God.

Pause.

We are entitled to wear these VIP badges – and so is everyone else, even people we don't like. In a moment of quiet, let's call to mind a person we find difficult, unlikeable or forgettable. They might annoy us or be unimportant to us. Perhaps we don't even remember their name.

Pause.

On the other side of your badge, name, draw or describe that person and write the same letters which appear under your name: 'VIP'.

Allow time for people to do this, then put on their badges.

37. Conference badges are available cheaply from eBay and other internet-based retailers, including Amazon. The 'VIP' message was inspired by Back to Church Sunday a few years ago. Resources included VIP balloons: any leftover stocks of these would complement this prayer.

Closing words

Lord of all,
we come before you, equally loved by you.
Help us to remember that we are all your children.
Amen.

New life

Resources
- Time-lapse film of growing plants[38] and equipment to show it on

Leader: Every spring we see new life begin to grow again, and this familiar miracle reminds us that God gives life to us all. He gave us this green and fertile planet and through Christ's death on the cross gave us all the gift of eternal life. For our prayers today, we will watch a piece of film that shows the wonder of new life. Let's rest in God's presence and give thanks.

Prayer action: Watch the time-lapse film and pause at the end.

Closing words: God of life,
we thank you for our sprouting, blooming,
teeming world,
evolving and ever new;
we thank you for your living and dying Son
whose death gave new life to us all.
Amen.

38. The best clip I have found is in the 1993 film of *The Secret Garden*. Find scene 18, 'Spring comes': it begins with a coach leaving in the dark, but then leads into lovely time-lapse footage of the garden bursting into life, accompanied by music. If you can't get hold of this, try the DVD of David Attenborough's *The Private Life of Plants* (BBC, 1995) or search the internet for time-lapse films (there are lots on YouTube).

Welcome mat

Resources

- 'Welcome' mat in front of the altar or table [39]
- *(Optional music)* 'People have Names' by Juliet Turner [40] and sound equipment to play it on

Leader

For our prayers today we will use this ordinary 'Welcome' mat. Some of us may have one just like this by our front door. Here, it is a reminder that God welcomes us all – whoever we are, wherever we've been. In a time of quiet, we will remember this. Take a moment to hold on to that welcome and thank God for it; ask him who else we could welcome in his name. If you would like to come forward and stand on the Welcome mat yourself, please do. Let us pray.

Prayer action

If you are using the music, start it now. Then stand on the Welcome mat yourself for a moment before encouraging anyone who wishes to do the same. Others may choose to remain seated. Give people time for reflection.

Closing words

Loving Lord,
you opened your arms in welcome on the cross.
May we accept your open invitation
and with open arms
may we welcome others in your name.
Amen.

39. Home hardware shops still sell the genuine article; alternatively, make a home-made version out of a carpet square with stuck-on felt letters.
40. This sweet and gentle song is well-worth using if you can get hold of it. It is on the album of the same name, which is available from Amazon.co.uk as a CD or MP3; the site also offers you the chance to hear a sample. The lyrics are particularly appropriate in this context:
    People have names, people have voices,
    people have stories that never get told . . .
    We need a sign on the door that says welcome,
    whoever you are, wherever you've been.

Sweet

Resources
- Several boxes of *After Eight* thin mints[41]
- Lots of small pieces of card that are the same size as the mints
- Pens and pencils in every pew or row of seats

Leader There is a mealtime grace that asks, 'For what we are about to receive, may the Lord make us truly thankful'. Our prayers today are all about thanksgiving and, to help us pray, we have something sweet to eat. First of all we will pass these boxes of chocolates around: please take one and enjoy it! As you do so, think of something good in your life for which you would like to thank God. Write or draw it on one of these little pieces of card, then put the card in the little black envelope that held your chocolate.

Prayer action *Pass the chocolate boxes around and allow plenty of time for people to eat and offer their prayers.*

Now let's collect all our prayers in the boxes that contained the chocolates. We will exchange our treats for thanksgivings.

Pass round the empty boxes and fill them up again with the little black envelopes, now containing prayers instead of chocolates.

Closing words Lord, for all that we have received, may you make us truly thankful.
Amen.

41. Don't buy supermarket 'own brand' after-dinner mints, unless you are sure they come with the little black envelopes – not all of them do. Thanks to my sweet-toothed daughter, Phoebe, for this lovely prayer idea!

Compass

Resources

- A large compass drawn on a piece of board: a simple face with four arms labelled N, S, E and W. Hold it up at the start of the prayer
- Tea lights
- Matches and tapers
- 2 prayer leaders

Leader

Jesus described himself as 'the way', not 'the destination': he calls us on a journey of faith. On this adventure we may not always be sure which path we should take, so today we will pray for a clear sense of direction. We begin in the dark: let's turn off the lights and put our hands over our eyes.

Prayer action

Switch the lights off. Everyone places their hands over their eyes. As you lead the prayer, another leader should lay the compass on the floor, place tea lights along each arm and start lighting them.

With our eyes still closed, let us pray.

All-seeing Lord,
we pray for understanding.
On our Godward journey through life,
may we see clearly the direction in which you are calling us.

Pause until all the candles are lit.

Let's open our eyes.

Everyone does so and sees the compass on the floor, its cross shape lit with candles.

Closing words

Lord of the way, the truth and the life,
as we follow your call out into the world,
may your love be our life's compass.
Amen.

Empty chair

Resources

- Two chairs: one placed squarely at the front, the other ready to be placed next to it

Leader

Jesus spent his life amongst those people who needed him most: the sick and suffering, the poor and oppressed and those who lived chaotic, messed-up lives. In our prayers today, we think of Jesus sitting down next to all those who need him most. Here is an empty chair. Take a moment to think of someone you know who is finding life hard at the moment. Imagine that person sitting here in this chair.

Pause, then place a second chair beside the first.

Now here is another chair. If Jesus were physically here today, he would sit down beside this person. He isn't – but we are. In a moment of quiet, let's pray for whoever we are picturing in the first chair, and pray for ourselves: how might we sit down next to this person? What could we do to keep them company?

Prayer action

Keep silence for a short time.

Closing words

Brother Christ,
you came as one of us
and sat down next to those who needed you most.
Be with us now as we try to follow your example
and keep us company, today and always.
Amen.

Seasonal prayers

Here are prayers for those special occasions when our congregations may be larger and more diverse than usual: the Christmas Eve Crib service is full of toddlers, Mothering Sunday brings in extra families and on Remembrance Sunday we welcome uniformed organisations of all ages, from the Rainbows to the Royal British Legion. These are wonderful opportunities to gather together a wide variety of people and introduce them to fresh ways of praying.

Such special occasions are particularly demanding for clergy and worship leaders who feel under pressure to offer exciting, innovative all-age worship. Time, energy and inspiration may all be in short supply. Clergy who use social networking sites such as Facebook and Twitter frequently post desperate pleas at these times, such as: 'Have got to produce informal intercessions for this week's Harvest Festival – help!' and 'Need visual/creative prayer for Mothering Sunday. Any ideas?' This book, and particularly this section of prayers, is for all those who find themselves in this position.

Advent
Hopes and fears

Resources

- A large pin board covered with the outline of the 'mystery Messiah' (on CD-ROM – *see appendix, p.120*)
- Small blank cards, plus two labelled 'Hopes' and 'Fears'
- Pens and pencils
- Drawing pins

Leader

Remember the carol, 'O little town of Bethlehem'? In the opening verse, we sing that 'the hopes and fears of all the years' were met in Bethlehem on the night of Jesus' birth. The Jewish people had been waiting through the centuries for God's chosen one, the Messiah, to unite their people and restore their fortunes. *(Indicate the 'mystery Messiah' outline.)* No one knew who this mystery Messiah would be or when he would come, but the hopes and fears of an entire nation were pinned on him.

Pin the cards labelled 'Hopes' and 'Fears' onto the outline of the Messiah, covering the question mark.

As we wait excitedly for Christmas, we remember all the people who pinned their hopes and fears on the coming Messiah. We know the Son of God who fleshed out this outline, and soon we will celebrate his birth. We can continue to bring our hopes and fears to him in prayer. In a moment of quiet, let's call to mind all those people and situations we would like to bring before God.

Pause.

When you are ready, come forward and write or draw your prayer, then pin it to this outline of Jesus, the Messiah.

Prayer action — Allow plenty of time for people to complete their prayers.

Closing words — Father, we bring you our hopes and fears
in the name of Jesus, our long-awaited Saviour.
Amen.

Christmas Eve – Crib service
Starlight

Resources
- Gold star shapes (on CD-ROM, *see appendix, p.121*)
- Lengths of ribbon for hanging the stars on the tree
- Pens and pencils

Leader
Jesus is the light of the world. When we pray, we can ask him to shine the light of his love wherever there is darkness. For our prayers today, let's remember all those people who are most in need of love this Christmas. We think of those we love; people we know; people we don't like; those who may have no one to pray for them. *(Pause.)* Let's each take a gold star shape and write or draw our prayers on it. When you have finished your star prayer, come and add it to the branches of the Christmas tree.

Prayer action
Allow plenty of time for people to complete their prayers. If the church is packed, it may be easier to collect the stars and bring them forward in collection plates, then invite a couple of helpers to hang them on the tree.

Closing words
Jesus, Light of the world,
we offer these prayers in your name.
Shine like a star in the darkness
and guide us all closer to you.
Amen.

Christmas Day
Light of the world

Resources
- Advent wreath, matches and tapers
- Hand-held votive candles, given to each person as they arrive

Leader *Turn out the lights.*

John's Gospel says this about Jesus: 'What has come into being in him was life, and the life was the light of all people. The light shines in the darkness, and the darkness did not overcome it.'[42] For our prayers today, we wait in the dark and remember all those known to us who need the light of Christ, especially in this Christmas season.

Prayer action *Pause. Light your own votive candle from the central candle of the Advent wreath.*

In Jesus was life, and the life was the light of all people.

Pass the light among the people. Pause once all the candles are lit.

Closing words Jesus, Light of the world,
shine on those for whom we pray
and give them new life.
May your inextinguishable light
burn in our hearts this Christmas
and every day.
Amen.

42. John 1:4-5.

Epiphany
Bethlehem sky

Resources
- A large piece of black card with a silver Star of Bethlehem in the centre
- Lots of gold and silver star stickers

Leader The wise men followed the star that led them to Jesus, but they can't have been the only people who were drawn to that strange, bright light in the sky. Ordinary people must have looked at it and wondered, hoped that it was a sign of their Saviour's coming. Our prayers today will focus on that bright Bethlehem star. Whatever it is you would like to bring before God, whoever you would like to pray for, come and add a little star to this sky as a sign of your prayer.

Prayer action Encourage people to come forward and add a star to the Bethlehem sky picture.

Closing words God of everything,
the prayers of your people are more than all the stars in the sky,
but your love is wider, longer, higher and deeper than space itself.
May each prayer hold its place in your heart,
in Jesus' name.
Amen.

Candlemas
Sweet and sour

Resources

- Several packets of the sweets called Skittles. You will need two varieties: regular Skittles and Skittles Sour
- Two bowls

Leader

Christ's presentation in the Temple is bittersweet[43] because it holds in one moment the joy of Jesus' birth and the pain of his death on the cross, as foretold by Simeon. Today we will pray edible, bittersweet prayers. As we rest quietly in God's presence, I will pass round two bowls of sweets: they look identical, but these are sweet *(show Bowl 1)* and these are sour *(show Bowl 2)*. As you taste sweetness, call to mind something good in your life and thank God for it. Then, as you taste sourness, call to mind something sad that you would like to bring to God in prayer. It may be a prayer for you, for someone you love or for people in the world who are suffering today. In this quiet time, let us pray.

Prayer action

Pass the bowls around and allow enough time for everyone to finish their prayers.

Closing words

Heavenly Father,
hear our bittersweet prayers
for the sake of your Son, Jesus Christ,
who was born and died for us.
Amen.

43. Luke 2:22-40. I am grateful to Amanda Evans, whose reflections on the bittersweetness of Candlemas inspired this sweet and sour prayer.

Ash Wednesday
Messy hands

Resources
- A tray of ashes mixed with a little water [44]
- A long strip of lining paper laid in front of the altar or table
- A couple of large bowls
- A couple of large jugs full of water
- Rolls of kitchen towel and a bin
- An assistant Prayer Leader (non-speaking)

Leader As Lent begins, we say sorry to God for all we have done wrong. In ancient times, people used to show that they were sad and sorry by covering themselves in ash. *(Show the tray of ashes.)* Christians used this symbol of penitence and mourning to make the sign of the cross on their foreheads at the beginning of Lent, which is why today became known as Ash Wednesday. Today we will use these ashes to make messy hand-prints. We will all make a print, because all of us – at some point in our lives – have made a mess of things. We may have said or done the wrong thing or failed to do the right thing. Come forward to leave your own ash handprint and, as you do so, call to mind something for which you would like to say, 'Sorry.' When you have finished, don't wipe your hands – we will wash them together as part of our prayers today.

44. The usual practice for traditional Ash Wednesday ashing is to burn last year's palm crosses. One cross yields enough ash to make the sign of the cross on about ten foreheads – clearly more will be needed to cover hands. Once the crosses have been reduced to ash, add a little water to make a dusty paste that will stick to hands more easily. Spread the paste onto a tray that has a raised rim. If the mixture still looks a little sparse, you could add some crumbled charcoal.

Prayer action *Make your own ash handprint first and encourage everyone else to do so.*

Here we all are with our messy, ashy hands. These are a physical reminder that none of us is perfect. We all need forgiveness for our sins. In the Bible, being forgiven is often compared to being washed clean, so today we will wash our hands as we pray for God's forgiveness. Let us pray.

The Prayer Leaders wash each other's hands first. Then invite everyone to come forward and wash their hands by holding them over a bowl as water is poured on them.

Closing words May you make in us a clean heart, O God,
and renew a right spirit within us,
in Jesus' name.
Amen.

Mothering Sunday
Prayer darts

Resources
- Large prayer dart template (instructions on CD-ROM, *see appendix, p.121*)
- A3 sheet of paper for the Leader
- In every pew or row of seats: A5 sheets of paper and pens

Leader The Bible describes what being a mother is like when it says that children are 'like arrows in the hand of a warrior.'[45] To shoot an arrow, you need to line it up, hold it carefully in place while you pull back the bowstring and then . . . let it go. In the same way, a mother's love has to both hold on and let go. She has to hold her children in love and guide them, but also let them have the freedom to go their own way – like arrows flying from a bow.

Our prayers today will take the shape of arrows, because prayer is also an act of holding on and letting go. We hold particular people and situations in our hearts; then we offer them to God, letting the prayer fly like an arrow. Take your time now to think about anything and anyone you wish to hold in prayer. Then write or draw your prayers on a sheet of paper.

45. Psalm 127:4.

Prayer action

Allow time for people to write or draw their prayers.

Now we will turn these pieces of paper into prayer darts: these are similar to paper aeroplanes but smaller and sharper, like arrow heads.[46]

Using the template and A3 paper, demonstrate how to fold the paper into a dart, but don't throw anything yet. When people are ready, invite them to stand.

Let's hold onto our prayer darts and get ready to throw them when I say, 'LET THEM GO.' Let us pray.

Motherly God,
we hold these prayers in our hearts
and we LET THEM GO to you.

Let all the prayer darts fly.

Closing words

In Jesus' name.
Amen.

Encourage the children to gather up all the prayer darts and place them on the altar or a table.

46. Paper aeroplanes feature in a Messy Church prayer (Lucy Moore, *Messy Church*, BRF, 2006), and have been discussed at length by Rebecca Nye as an expression of Godly Play's 'wondering' (Ed. Anne Richards and Peter Privett, *Through the Eyes of a Child*, Church House Publishing, 2009). In my version, the darts are inspired by the description of urgent supplication as an 'arrow prayer.'

Palm Sunday
Passion

Resources
- Unleavened bread and a goblet or plain chalice
- A Roman sword (available from English Heritage outlets or toy shops)
- A purple cloak and a crown of thorns
- A large wooden cross
- A wooden mallet and some long nails
- A white sheet

Leader The Easter story is for everyone: it is real and relevant to all of us. On Easter Day it will be time to tell the happy ending. For now, let's rest in God's presence and reflect on these objects from the Passion story we have told again today *(lay them down as you name them)*: Passover bread and wine; a soldier's sword; a royal cloak and a crown of thorns; a rough wooden cross; a mallet and nails; a shroud. You may like to come up and hold some of these or look at them more closely. In a moment of quiet, ask God to speak to you through these things. Let us pray.

Prayer action Keep silence for a short time. People may like to come up and hold the objects as they pray.

Closing words Son of God,
this week may we walk with you
through the story of your Passion.
May we praise you with Hosannas
and remember that it is our sins that cry 'Crucify!'
Make us witnesses of your sacrifice,
for your love's sake.
Amen.

Maundy Thursday
Bitter herbs

Resources
- Some bitter herbs such as parsley, rosemary, romaine lettuce or endive
- Words and music for the Taizé chant, 'Within our darkest night'[47]

Leader
For our prayers today, we will use some bitter herbs. In the Passover meal, which was Jesus' Last Supper, herbs like these represent the bitterness of human suffering. As we sing the Taizé chant, 'Within our darkest night,' we will take some bitter herbs, smell or taste them and remember how Jesus suffered for our sake. We also remember all those who suffer in body, mind and spirit. We bring our own suffering before God. Let us pray.

Prayer action
Pass the herbs around and pause for a short time of silence. Then begin singing the chant, softly at first. Repeat until everyone has taken some herbs and had an opportunity to pray.

Closing words
Lord Jesus,
however dark our night,
however bitter our pain,
may we trust in you,
source of all light and life.
Amen.

47. This chant can be found in *Hymns Old & New*, also published by Kevin Mayhew Ltd.

Good Friday
Pierced heart

Resources
- A rough wooden cross, a claw hammer and a nail
- A pile of paper hearts[48]

Leader *Bring forward the wooden cross with the pile of hearts nailed to the centre.*

In John's Gospel, there is a beautiful description of Jesus' love for us: 'Having loved his own who were in the world, he loved them to the end.'[49] Here is a visual symbol of that love: a heart, pierced by suffering and loss, which keeps on loving to the end. For our prayers today, let's take a heart to keep as a symbol of Jesus' love for us. In a time of quiet, we will ask him to show us how to love one another as he has loved us.

Prayer action Take out the nail and pass around the pierced hearts. Pause for a moment of quiet.

Closing words Loving Lord,
may your love be the heartbeat of our lives,
animating all that we say and do.
Amen.

48. Newsagents and pound shops often sell heart-shaped sticky notes or memo pads. These would be ideal as they stay together in the shape of one heart.
49. John 13:1.

Easter Day
Sparklers

Resources

- A bonfire or brazier outside the church, around which everyone gathers
- Sparklers[50]

Leader

On this Easter day, we bear witness to the reality of Jesus' life after death. We rejoice that he died and rose again for us so that we might leave all our old ways behind us, all our mistakes and wrongdoing, and find new, real and eternal life in Christ. For our prayers today, we light these sparklers as beacons to celebrate the good news of Easter. The response to each prayer intention is, 'We praise you.' Let us pray.

Prayer action

Hand out the sparklers and light them from each other.

Almighty God,
for your Son, who blazed a trail
that leads us to you,
we praise you.
For his life, death and resurrection
we praise you.
For the gift of eternal life,
we praise you.

Closing words

Amen.

When the sparklers have gone out, throw them onto the bonfire.

50. Many toy shops sell these all year round. Alternatively, there are lots of internet sites that sell fireworks out of season.

Ascension
Cloud of unknowing[51]

Resources

- Small pictures of clouds (on CD-ROM, *see appendix, p.121*)
- Pens and pencils

Leader

In medieval pictures of the Ascension, the disciples are often shown looking upwards with their mouths open in astonishment. In front of their eyes, Christ is disappearing into a miraculous cloud that takes him up to heaven. Of course they are amazed – but they look baffled, too. Gawping like landed fish, they seem to be thinking, 'What's happening? What do we do now?'

If we stop to think about it, we know what this mixture of awe and confusion feels like. We are surrounded by things that we don't fully understand: things that are too big (such as the universe) or too small (such as sub-atomic particles) or too complex (such as our planet's ecosystem). God himself is the most wonderful and mysterious of all. For our prayers today, we will bring before God some of those things that astonish and baffle us. We will use these clouds, like the one that took Jesus back up into heaven. Take one and write or draw on it whatever it is that you find hard to understand.

Prayer action

Allow time for everyone to complete their prayers. Encourage people to bring their clouds forward and leave them on the altar or table.

51. This is the title of an anonymous medieval guide to contemplative prayer. The author recommends that, since God is beyond our intellectual comprehension, we should suspend all thoughts, words and ideas in prayer and simply love God. He describes this as piercing the 'cloud of unknowing' that is between us and God with the 'sharp dart of longing love'.

Closing words

Heavenly Father,
we surrender to you all the things that are
beyond our comprehension:
hold our wonder, confusion and questioning
in your hands.
May we look for you in love within this cloud
of unknowing,
trusting that you are here
and your Spirit is with us.
Amen.

Pentecost
Sky lanterns

Resources
- Sky lanterns[52]
- Matches
- Felt pens

Leader Our Pentecost prayers will be prayers for change: we will make them using flying lanterns that are powered by fire. Paper sky lanterns like these were used in ancient Chinese celebrations. Once the flame beneath them has been lit, they rise up into the air and float for as long as the flame burns.

Today we will cover these lanterns with our prayers before releasing them into the sky. Let's take a moment to call to mind all those who need the Holy Spirit's wind of change to blow into their lives: we remember political disagreements that have reached stalemate, relationships that are stuck in a rut or people known to us who want to leave their old ways behind them. *(Pause.)* When you are ready, gather round a lantern and write or draw your prayers on it.

Prayer action Encourage people to come forward and cover the lanterns with their prayers. When everyone is ready, take the lanterns outside, light the fuel and release them. As you watch them float away, say the following words.

52. These are becoming widely available: I have seen them in toy shops such as Hawkin's Bazaar and even in a local newsagents. They make a spectacular display if launched together, especially at night. Most sky lanterns are quite large, so a pack of ten should provide plenty of space for people to write their prayers. For a daytime service like this one, you may like to buy coloured lanterns. The internet is probably your best source, especially if you are concerned about the environment: fully bio-degradable, metal-free sky lanterns are now available. For example, see www.skylanterns4u.co.uk.

Closing words

Let us pray.

Holy Spirit, Wind of change,
may you lift these prayers to God our Father
in Jesus' name.
Amen.

Trinity
Three-in-One

Resources
- Glowsticks and connectors[53]

Leader On this Trinity Sunday, we celebrate the mystery of our God, the Three-in-One. He is God the Father, God the Son and God the Holy Spirit – three persons yet one indivisible God. As a sign of our prayers today, we will make three interlinked circles of light. *(Demonstrate the following actions as you talk.)* Take three glowsticks and bend them to make them glow. Use a connector to make the first ring; then make a second ring which links through the first. Finally, make a third ring which links through the other two. As we join these circles of light together, we rest in God's presence and remember that he is eternally Three yet always One. Let us pray.

Prayer action Allow plenty of time for people to make their interlinked rings.

Closing words God our Maker,
Christ our Mender,
Holy Spirit, Mover and Shaker,
three Persons of the one God,
be with us now and always.
Amen.

53. These are thin plastic sticks that contain a coloured chemical that becomes fluorescent when the stick is flexed. They are available from toy shops, pound shops and many newsagents. Each pack also contains a number of small plastic connectors that can be used to form sticks into rings. See also www.glowsticks.co.uk.

Fathers' Day
Team shirt

Resources
- 'Jesus' team shirt' cards (on CD-ROM, *see appendix, p.122*)

Leader
On Fathers' Day we celebrate the bond between dads and their children. When it is strong and loving, nothing can take away that feeling of belonging. We call God 'our Father' because he loves us like this: whoever we are and whatever we've done, we are counted among his children. It's like having a place on his team that he will never take away from us. To remind us of this, our prayer today features a gift. *(Hold up your 'Jesus' team shirt' card.)* This is Jesus' team shirt![54] These cards are shaped like loyalty cards to remind us that Jesus wants you, me and all of us to be on his team. In a moment of quiet, please take a card and think about what this might mean for you.

Prayer action
Encourage people to come forward and take a card. Pause for a short time.

Closing words
Fatherly God,
we thank you for dads.
Whether we are fathers, sons or daughters,
may we accept our place on your team
in Jesus' name.
Amen.

Please keep this card in your wallet or purse to remind you of Jesus' invitation.

54. Optional joke, depending on your congregation: Why is it a goalie's shirt? Because Jesus saves!

Harvest
Feast and famine

Resources

- A very large map of the world[55]
- A small plastic bowl full of plain cooked brown rice
- A tray with two plates – a hearty ploughman's lunch on one and a slice of cake on the other

Leader

For our prayers today, we will gather round this map of the world to reflect on real food as we remember those with little and those with plenty.

Encourage everyone to gather around the world map.

Let us pray.

God, our generous Creator,
at this harvest time we pray for your world.

Prayer action

Place the bowl of plain brown rice over a part of the world that is currently experiencing famine.

We pray for the people who will eat this today, but won't eat again until tomorrow or next week.

Place the tray with a ploughman's lunch and a slice of cake over a wealthy part of the world.

We pray for the people who will eat this for lunch, between breakfast, dinner and snacks.

Closing words

God of all good things,
shower us with your blessings
and teach us how to share.
Amen.

55. A great resource is the giant, brightly coloured plastic floor mat in the children's game, 'Globe Trotting', produced by the Early Learning Centre. If you can't get hold of this, you could stick some large pieces of card or lining paper together and paint on the continents and countries with a thick brush.

All Saints
Joined hands

Resources This is a resource-free prayer.

Leader In Christ, we are members of one family. Our prayers join together with the prayers of Christians across the world and the saints in heaven. Today we remember that we are never alone when we pray. Rather than putting our own hands together, let's join hands with the people next to us, as we sometimes do on New Year's Eve when we sing 'Auld Lang Syne'. We will stand with joined hands and, in a moment of quiet, each bring our own prayer before God. Let us pray.

Prayer action Encourage everyone to cross and link hands around the church. Pause for a short time.

Closing words Lord of all,
we pray with each other,
in communion with the saints
and in the name of your Son, Jesus Christ;
O Lord, hear our prayer.
Amen.

All Souls
Prayer window

Resources

- A clear window: make a simple arched window frame out of stiff black card and fill it with a sheet of clear plastic.[56] It needs to be big enough for several people to write on it at once
- Brightly coloured permanent markers ('Sharpie' pens come in a wide range of colours)

Leader

Many churches have stained-glass windows that are memorials to people who have died. In our prayers today, we will colour this window with the names of those we have lost, as a mark of our remembrance and a sign of our prayer. Let's remember those known to us who have died.

Prayer action

Using a coloured permanent marker, write a name on the clear plastic window, then allow plenty of time for people to come forward and write the names of those they wish to remember. When the window is covered with colour, hold it up in front of the candlelit altar or table.

Closing words

Almighty God,
may the light of your love
shine upon these souls
and upon those who mourn,
in Jesus' name.
Amen.

56. Many garden centres and hardware shops sell heavy-duty plastic sheeting by the yard: this would be ideal.

Remembrance Sunday
Peace poppies[57]

Resources

- Seven big white paper poppies (on CD-ROM, *see appendix, p.122*). Number these 1–7 on the back and give them out to members of your congregation. Explain that after each prayer, they will bring their poppies forward in turn and lay them down to form the shape of the cross

Leader

Today we remember those who have died in conflict and we pray for peace. We will use these white poppies, which are a symbol of peace. (*Invite the volunteers to stand and hold up their poppies.*) After each prayer, there will be a pause as a poppy is brought forward. In that time of quiet, we will offer our own prayers in silence. When I say, 'Father, we pray,' please respond, 'Peace be upon them.' If you are one of those for whom we pray, please respond, 'Peace be upon us.' Let us pray.

Prayer action

God of peace,
for all those who have died in conflict,

Pause. The first poppy is brought forward and laid down.

Father, we pray:
peace be upon them.

For all those who have been injured by war in body, mind or spirit,

Pause. The second poppy is brought forward and laid down.

57. The white 'peace poppy' can be controversial when worn instead of the red poppy, because it may be seen as an anti-military, pacifist statement. In this context, where people will presumably be wearing red poppies and laying wreaths of red poppies as usual, the white poppy should be an acceptable symbol of our prayers for peace.

Father, we pray:
peace be upon them.

For all those who fight for justice and freedom today,

Pause. The third poppy is brought forward and laid down.

Father, we pray:
peace be upon them.

For the families who mourn or wait in hope and fear,

Pause. The fourth poppy is brought forward and laid down.

Father, we pray:
peace be upon them.

For all the ordinary people killed, injured and made homeless by war,

Pause. The fifth poppy is brought forward and laid down.

Father, we pray:
peace be upon them.

For those in power whose names can summon armies or sign peace treaties,

Pause. The sixth poppy is brought forward and laid down.

Father, we pray:
peace be upon them.

For the local peacemakers and peacekeepers,

Pause. The seventh poppy is brought forward and laid down, completing the shape of the cross.

Father, we pray:
peace be upon them.

Closing words We ask this in the name of Jesus Christ,
the Prince of Peace.
Amen.

Patronal Festival
Unbroken circle

Resources

This is a resource-free prayer.

Leader

Today we celebrate the fact that God's love joins us together. We belong to this church and to the Church across the world, and we are connected to our patron saint *(insert name)* and all the saints who pray for us in heaven. Together, we belong to the family of God. In our prayers today, we pray for our togetherness by gathering in a circle and linking hands.

Prayer action

Encourage everyone to form a circle and hold hands. Practise the two moves needed for this prayer: a wide circle, with arms stretched out, and a tighter circle, formed by everyone moving towards the middle (as in the Hokey Cokey). Begin the prayer with a wide circle.

Let us pray.

Lord of love,
teach us to work together
and help each other
like partners in a dance.

Lead the circle inwards, to form a tighter circle.

Closing words

Whatever our differences,
may your love be the music
that brings us closer.
Amen.

Appendix
CD-ROM contents and instructions

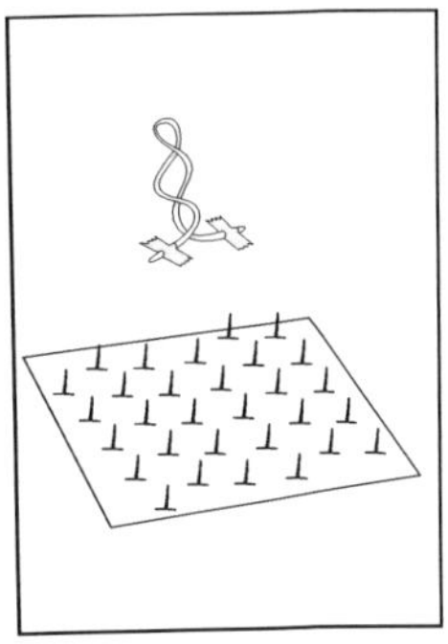

Tray prepared for the prayer plants
(*Prayer plants*, p.23)
The prayer plants need some support so that people can 'plant' them upright. Try using lots of pipe-cleaners, twisted and then sellotaped down, like this. Then cover a tray or piece of board with twists so that each prayer plant may be placed over a twist.

Template for prayer plants
(*Prayer plants*, p.23)
Make a couple of copies on A4 card for people to follow as they make their own with green paper. Demonstrate how to 'grow' the finished plants by pinching the very end of the paper rolled inside the cylinder and pulling upwards, so that the thin leaves spread outwards.

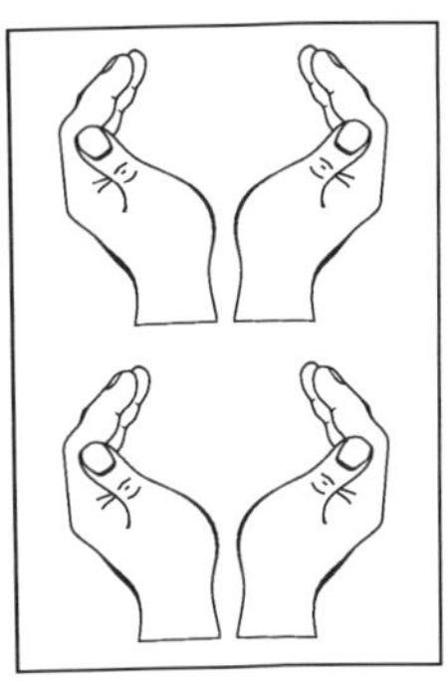

Cards with cupped hands
(*He holds us in his hands*, p.25)
Copy onto A4 card and cut into two A5 pieces. Make enough for one each.

Template for X-ray specs

(*X-ray specs*, p.26)

Make copies on coloured card, enough for one each.

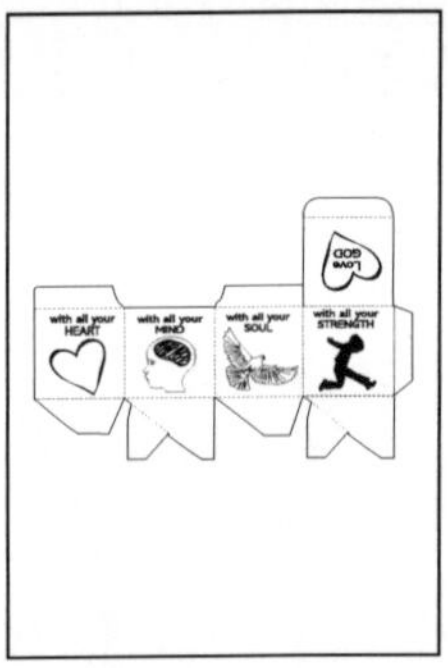

Net for the prayer cube

(*Prayer cube*, p.27)

Copy enough for one each onto A4 card. Cut out along the solid lines then fold along the dotted lines to form the cube, securing with double-sided sticky tape on the tabs. Make one for a demonstration model: fold it into a cube but don't stick it together, so that during the prayer you can show how it works.

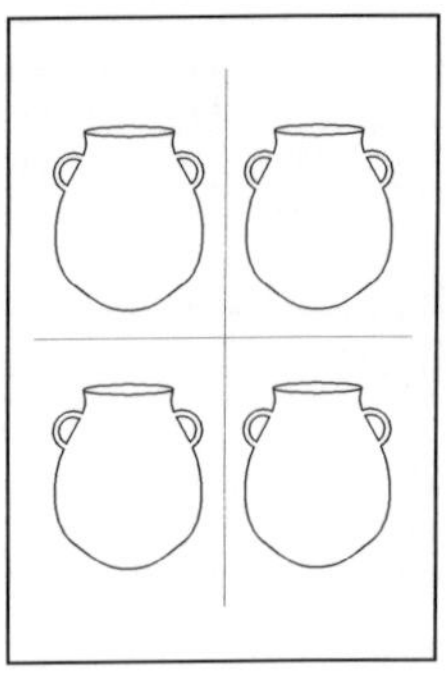

Pictures of stone water jars

(*Water jars*, p.36)

Make several copies on A4 paper and cut along the straight solid lines.

Question mark cards

(*Questions*, p.37)

Make several copies on A4 paper and cut along the straight solid lines.

Shaped cards
(*Bright and beautiful*, p.38)
Make several copies on A4 card in different colours, then cut out the shapes.

Jesus the good shepherd
(*Lost sheep*, p.40)
Make a large copy of the picture, either by hand or by photocopying and enlarging in sections. Mount the finished picture on a large, stiff piece of card. Leave plenty of room for the lambs to be placed around him.

Cards with the outline of a lamb
(*Lost sheep*, p.40)
Make several copies on A4 paper and cut along the straight solid lines.

Cards with a crown

(*Gift*, p.73)

Make double-sided copies on A4 card, cut out and laminate if possible. Then wrap up each card in gift wrapping.

Hearts cut out of red card

(*Heart*, p.80)

Make several copies on red A4 card and cut out the hearts.

'Mystery Messiah' outline

(*Christmas Eve*, p.90)

Print out one copy and enlarge by hand or with a photocopier. Make it as large as possible.

Gold star shapes

(*Christmas Eve*, p.92)

Copy on A4 gold card or paper and cut out. Use a hole punch for the hole.

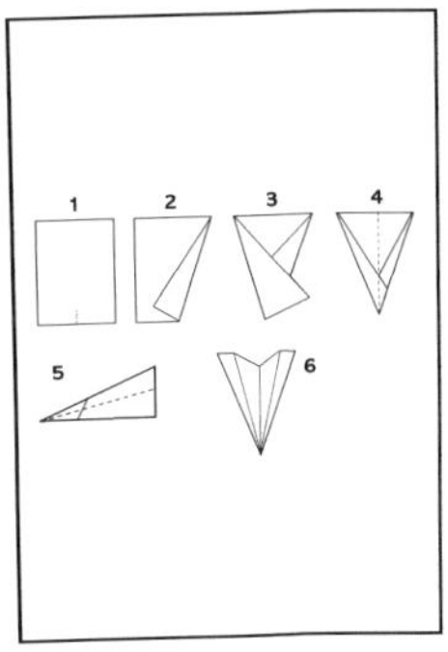

Prayer dart instructions

(*Mothering Sunday*, p.98)

Print off a few copies of the instructions for reference. Demonstrate with A3 paper (the congregation will use A5). The aim is to produce a dart rather than an aeroplane, so keep it simple, for example:

1. Mark the mid-point on one short side.
2. Make a long diagonal fold to the mid-point.
3. Make a second diagonal fold, tucking the overhanging point behind the dart.
4. Fold the whole dart lengthways.
5. Starting at the point, fold back the wings.
6. The finished dart.

Small pictures of clouds

(*Ascension*, p.104)

Make several copies on A4 paper and cut along the straight solid lines.

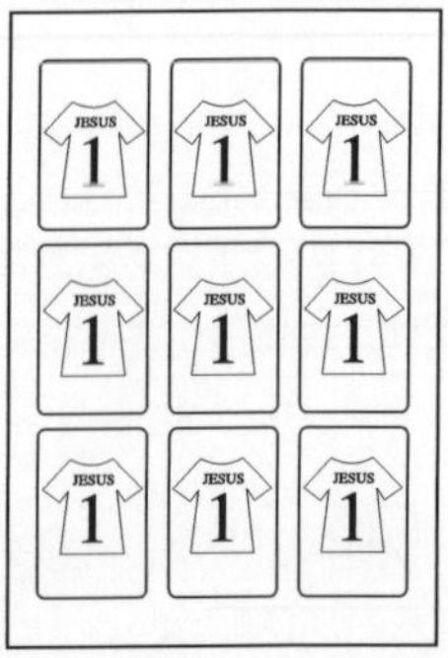

'Jesus' team shirt' cards
(*Fathers' Day*, p.109)
Copy on white A4 card and cut out. Make enough for one each.

White poppies
(*Remembrance*, p.113)
Make two copies on white A4 card and cut out.

Also by Claire Benton-Evans

All-Sorts Prayer
Creative Prayers for all ages

A unique opportunity to unite people of all ages and abilities in prayer. The prayers are grouped by theme and suggested position in the service and each lists resources needed, words for the leader, a prayer action and closing words. Instructions are given for those who require them and the CD-ROM provides many of the resources.

Product code: 1501223

Encountered
Meeting God in Ordinary Places –
A Lent course

Five sessions exploring the ordinary places of the Easter story in which the extraordinary events of Jesus' life, death and resurrection occurred.

Product code: 1501200

Revealed
A course uncovering Advent to Epiphany (Based on *Calendar Girls* and *The Full Monty*)

Six sessions, taking themes from film scenes and applying them to the Bible, exploring ways in which we are revealed to ourselves and to God, and how God reveals himself to us and to the world.

Product code: 1501198

Food for Prayer
Tempting ideas for daily nourishment

Fireworks, blackberrying, Doctor Who, saints' feet, spring tides, James Bond, pantomimes – all and more have inspired the prayers within this new book.

Product code: 1501142